Table of Contents

Love Beyond Death

Introduction

Chapter 1 : The Beginning Of Love

Chapter 2 : Building A Life Together

Chapter 3 : A Love That Inspired Others — Ordinary Yet Extraordinary

Chapter 4 : The Sudden Loss

Chapter 5 : The Day The World Stopped

Chapter 6 : The Void

Chapter 7 : Finding A New Path In His Memory

Chapter 8 : Rediscovering Myself

Chapter 9 :The Love That Never Fades

A Love Letter To My Heavenly Husband

A Note To The Reader

About The Author

LOVE BEYOND DEATH

Finding Grace in the Face of Heartache

To my beloved husband, Yatin

This book, Love Beyond Death, is a tribute to you, to us, and to the love that transcends time and space.

Through the unpredictable journey of life, you were my anchor, my joy, and my greatest blessing. Even in your absence, your presence fills every moment of my days, teaching me that true love never ends—it evolves, it deepens, and it guides.

This is our story: of meeting, of love, of loss, and of acceptance. It is my way of honoring you and the life we shared. Your memory inspires me to embrace life with grace, strength, and gratitude.

Forever yours,

Apurva

INTRODUCTION

Life is a journey full of surprises—some that fill our hearts with joy and others that challenge us in ways we could never imagine. Love Beyond Death is a story of one such journey, my journey, with the most beautiful soul I have ever known—my husband, Yatin.

This book is a reflection on how life's unpredictability led me to face the greatest loss of my existence with grace and acceptance.

Death is not the end of love. Love continues to grow, evolve, and heal, even when the person you love is no longer physically by your side.

Through Love Beyond Death, I share my personal experiences—our love story, the moments that defined us, and the lessons I learned about life, loss, and resilience. My hope is that this book will inspire others to embrace their own journeys with courage, to find peace amidst pain, and to believe in the enduring power of love.

This is not just my story; it is a story for anyone who has loved deeply, lost profoundly, and yet continues to live with an open heart.

With love,

Apurva

Chapter 1 : The Beginning Of Love

This story is about how me and Yatin met, a tale of serendipity and spiritual connection. enlightenment.

I stood in the auditorium, my voice carrying the wisdom of ages as I explained the significance of Sadguru and rituals. My passion and deep understanding captivated audience, weaving a spell of awe and reverence. Among the listeners was Yatin, a young man whose curiosity about the spiritual world had brought him to this sacred place.

Yatin's eyes were drawn to me, not just because of my knowledge but also because of the calm radiance I exuded. I seemed like the embodiment of the serenity he had been searching for. Determined to know more about me, he tried to approach me after the session, but my polite smile and quick departure left him standing there, uncertain.

For the rest of the retreat, Yatin found himself gravitating toward her sessions, hanging on to every word I spoke. He tried to initiate conversations in the meditation hall, and even during communal meals, but I remained distant, focused on her duties and her own spiritual path.

Despite her apparent indifference, Yatin didn't give up. He admired my dedication and the quiet strength I seemed to carry. Slowly, his persistence began my example.

One evening, Yatin found an opportunity to speak from the heart. He approached me with humility. "Your words have helped me see things differently," he said softly. "I just wanted to thank you for that."

I paused, my gaze meeting his for the first time with genuine interest. There was sincerity in his tone that I couldn't ignore. "I'm glad," I replied, my voice carrying a warmth he hadn't heard before. "That's why I'm here—to share what I've learned. If it's helped you, then it's worth it."

From that moment, a subtle shift occurred. Yatin's focus remained on his spiritual growth, and I began to notice the sincerity of his efforts. Our conversations grew from fleeting exchanges to meaningful discussions about faith, purpose of life. I who had once viewed him as a distraction, started to see him as a kindred spirit.

I admitted, "I didn't expect to connect with anyone here. This place has always been about solitude for me."

Yatin smiled. "Sometimes, connections find us when we least expect them. Maybe it's part of the journey."

Our bond deepened with each passing day. I found myself drawn to his persistence, kindness, and the depth of his heart.

"Thank you for not giving up on me," I said, my voice filled with emotion.

"Thank you for letting me in," Yatin replied, taking her hand.

Under the serene glow of the temple, they made a silent promise to walk this path together, wherever it might lead.

"Love is the sunrise of the soul, where every dawn feels like the beginning of a life anew."

◆◆◆

Chapter 2 : Building A Life Together

Our wedding was full of magic . The air was filled with the aroma of fresh flowers and the soft hum of sacred chants, creating an atmosphere of peace and joy.

As we exchanged garlands and vowed to walk life's path together, I couldn't help but marvel at the serendipity that had brought us together. Yatin, holding her gaze, whispered, "This is just the beginning of our greatest adventure."

The Spiritual Bond

From the moment we tied the knot of our marriage, we both believed that marriage was not just a union of two people but a sacred journey of the soul.

Mornings in our home began with the soft chime of temple bells and the smell of incense wafting through the air. Together, we would sit for a short prayer, thanking the universe for its blessings and setting intentions for the day ahead.

Yatin often joked, "Our prayers are like coffee for the soul."

I would smile, holding his hand. "And you're my constant source of energy."

A Life Full of Love and Growth

Our days were filled with the little joys of life—cooking meals together, taking long evening walks, and spending hours lost in conversation. Yatin's love for sketching found a partner in poetry, and soon, our home was filled with art and verses that spoke of love, hope, and the beauty of life.

During one such trip, we found ourselves at a mountaintop ashram, where we meditated under the stars. That night, Yatin said, "When I'm with you, I feel closer to the universe. Like we're a part of something infinite."

Apurva placed her head on his shoulder and whispered, “That’s because love is infinite, Yatin. And ours will always be.”

"Brick by brick, love lays the foundation; trust cements it, and dreams build the walls of forever."

◆◆◆

Chapter 3 : A Love That Inspired Others – Ordinary Yet Extraordinary

Our relationship became a source of inspiration for friends and family. We believed in leading by example, showing that love wasn't just about grand gestures but about being present, patient, and understanding.

One of my favorite rituals was our yearly anniversary trip to a peaceful retreat. It would reflect on the past year, express gratitude for our hared journey, and set intentions.

A Spiritual Legacy

As the years passed, we continued to nurture our love, creating a life filled with meaning and beauty. Our home became a sanctuary, not just for ourselves but for anyone who visited—a place where laughter echoed, candles flickered, and love was always in the air.

On one quiet evening, we sat watching the sunset from the balcony, Yatin turned to me and said, "If I could live a thousand lifetimes, I'd choose you in every one of them."

I smiled, heart full. "And I'd find you, every time."

Together, we knew that our love was more than a fleeting moment in time—it was a spiritual connection, a bond that would last forever.

Through Life's Challenges

Life wasn't always smooth, but our bond only grew stronger with every challenge we faced. When Yatin had a difficult time at work, I reminded him to breathe and trust the process of universe by saying "Nothing is a curse , Everything is

Blessing" , When I struggled with self-doubt, Yatin became my biggest cheerleader, always encouraging me to follow my dreams.

We made it a point to never let the small worries of life overshadow the joy they found in each other.

“Every moment we spend together is a gift,” Yatin once said, holding me close after a particularly stressful day. “I never want to take that for granted.

"Our love, like a quiet flame, burned steady and strong—ordinary in its simplicity, extraordinary in its warmth."

◆◆◆

Chapter 4 : The Sudden Loss

The rhythmic clatter of the train wheels against the tracks echoed through the silent night as we traveled from Vaishno Devi to Mumbai. The gentle rocking of the compartment had lulled Yatin and our five-year-old daughter into a peaceful sleep. I remember watching them before I drifted off—Yatin's arm protectively draped over her small frame, her head nestled against his chest. It was a picture of serenity, a moment of calm in the whirlwind of our lives.

I awoke to her voice, a frantic cry piercing the stillness of the night. "Aai Aai" . Her small hands shook him as panic laced her words. Disoriented, I sat up, thinking it was his foot—a cramp, perhaps, or maybe he had shifted awkwardly in his sleep. But as I moved closer, something inside me froze. His body was still, unnaturally so, and his face bore an eerie calmness that didn't feel right.

"Yatin," I whispered, shaking him gently at first, then with increasing urgency. "Yatin, wake up. Please, wake up." There was no response. The world seemed to tilt, the train's motion amplifying the dread settling in my chest.

I grabbed his wrist, searching for a pulse. My hands trembled as I felt his skin, still warm but unyielding. My mind refused to accept what my heart already knew.

"Help! Someone help!" I screamed, my voice breaking as I clutched Yatin's hand. The compartment came alive with movement as fellow passengers stirred and rushed to our berth. Someone checked his pulse, another tried to administer CPR. The urgency in their actions mirrored the chaos in my mind, but deep down, a part of me knew we were too late.

When the train stopped at the next station, paramedics were waiting. They carried him away on a stretcher, my daughter and I trailing behind, her tiny hand clutching mine tightly. I clung to the hope that he could still be saved, that the man who had been my rock, my partner, my everything, would open his eyes and smile at me again.

But that moment never came. The doctor's words were a blur, their finality crashing over me like a wave. Cardiac arrest, they said. Sudden and swift. By the time we reached the hospital, he was already gone.

I sat in the sterile hospital room, numb and hollow, holding our daughter close as she sobbed into my chest. The weight of what had happened pressed down on me, suffocating and relentless. I replayed the night over and over in my mind, searching for a sign I might have missed, a moment where I could have changed the outcome. But there was nothing. Just the silence of the train, the cries of our daughter, and the unbearable reality of a world without Yatin.

I hadn't even said goodbye. Not a single word. The last conversation we had was about mundane things—tickets, snacks, our plans once we reached Mumbai. I hadn't told him how much he meant to me, how much I loved him. And now, I never could.

In the days that followed, I found myself reaching for him in moments of habit—to share a thought, to seek his advice, to feel his comforting presence. Each time, the emptiness was a cruel reminder of his absence.

But amidst the pain, I also found fragments of strength. In my daughter's laughter, in the memories we had built together, in the love he had left behind. Yatin's life, though cruelly cut short, was a testament to kindness, resilience, and devotion. He had given us so much to hold on to, even in his absence.

"His absence is a shadow cast by love's brightest light, a sudden silence where his laughter once echoed forever."

◆◆◆

Chapter 5 : The Day The World Stopped

The day Yatin left, my world stopped spinning.

It was a morning like any other. Everything was ordinary—deceptively so. I remember Yatin's laugh echoing in the hallway as he teased me about my mismatched socks, his voice a melody I had taken for granted. And then, like a candle snuffed out by an unseen gust, he was gone.

In the days that followed, time became meaningless. The clocks ticked, but their hands seemed frozen, mocking me with their relentless monotony. The world outside continued to move, oblivious to the gaping chasm that had opened in my chest. People came and went, offering their condolences in hushed tones, their words a cacophony of pity and discomfort. I nodded, thanked them, but their voices were distant, as if I were hearing them through a thick fog.

Yatin was everywhere and nowhere. His shoes by the door, the jacket he always forgot to hang, the half-finished book on the nightstand. Each object was a fragment of him, a shard of a life abruptly shattered. I found myself reaching for my phone to text him, to share a thought, a joke, only to be struck by the cruel reminder that he would never reply.

Grief is a peculiar thing. It’s not linear or predictable. Some days, I managed to get out of bed, to eat, to breathe without feeling like I was drowning. Other days, the weight of his absence was unbearable, and I would find myself sitting in the dark, clutching one of his shirts, inhaling the faint remnants of his scent.

As the weeks turned into months, the world began to seep back in, tentative and cautious. The pain didn’t lessen; it simply became a part of me, an ache that ebbed and flowed but never truly left. I started to find fragments of solace in the memories—the way Yatin’s eyes lit up when he talked about his dreams, the way his hand fit perfectly in mine, the way he made the ordinary extraordinary.

One day, I found a letter tucked into the pages of his journal. It wasn’t addressed to me, but I knew it was meant for me. In his familiar scrawl, he had written:
*"Life is fleeting, unpredictable, and sometimes cruel. But it is also beautiful in its fragility. Love fiercely, live boldly, and know that even when I’m gone, I’ll always be with you—in the wind, the stars, and the quiet moments in between."

Tears blurred my vision as I read those words, but for the first time since he left, I felt a flicker of something other than despair. It wasn’t hope, not yet, but it was a step toward it. Yatin’s words became my anchor, a reminder that even in the depths of loss, love endures.

The world hasn’t started spinning again, not fully. But I’ve learned to move with it, to find a fragile balance between holding on and letting go. Yatin’s absence is a wound that will never completely heal, but his presence—in my memories, my heart, and the life we shared—is a light that will never fade.

"The world stood still, as if even time bowed in sorrow, marking the moment when a heart was torn in two."

◆◆◆

Chapter 6 : The Void

On 17Dec2023,when Yatin passed away, it was as if the ground beneath me disappeared, and I fell into a void, a vast emptiness that consumed everything—my thoughts, my breath, my sense of self. The loss was so profound, so all-encompassing, that it felt as if a part of me had been ripped away, leaving me unrecognizable, a shadow of who I once was. I would reach for my phone, half-expecting to see a message from Yatin, only to be met with the harsh reality that I would never hear from him again. And each time, the weight of that truth would crash over me, suffocating, relentless.

My identity, once so certain, had been shattered. I had always been someone defined by the love I shared with him, someone who lived for our future together, who dreamed of building a life with him. But now, that future had crumbled, leaving me adrift in a sea of confusion. Who was I without him? What was the point of anything without the person who had made every moment meaningful? My reflection in the mirror seemed foreign, as if I were looking at a stranger who had no purpose, no direction. The person I had been before his death was lost to me, replaced by someone uncertain, fragile, broken.

Every routine, every part of my day, felt empty without him. The mornings that we used to share, waking up together and exchanging sleepy smiles, now felt hollow. I would drag myself out of bed, unable to find the energy to do anything but the bare minimum.

My meals were no longer something to look forward to, but just a task to get through. I would sit at the table, eating in silence, and feel the weight of his absence like a heavy, invisible presence beside me. I tried to carry on, to do the things I had always done, but they no longer held any meaning. The world felt like a muted version of itself, as if the colors had faded, and everything was seen through a fog.

The future, once full of possibilities, now seemed like a vast, unknowable void. How could I plan for tomorrow when I didn't even know who I was today? The dreams we had shared, the plans we had made, were no longer mine to chase. They were just memories, beautiful and painful, scattered like pieces of a puzzle that would never fit together again.

I couldn't picture a life without him in it, couldn't imagine a path forward that didn't lead to the place where he should have been standing beside me.

Yet, amid the confusion, the grief, and the sense of being lost, something began to stir deep inside me. It wasn't hope, not yet, but a faint glimmer of something else—something that felt like a whisper, like Yatin's presence was still with me, urging me to move forward. I didn't know how or when, but slowly, I started to pick up the pieces of my life, one by one. The void, while still present, began to feel less suffocating. It was as though I was learning to live in the space he had left behind, not to fill it with distractions or false promises, but to allow it to become a part of me, a space that would always carry his memory, his love.

I didn't have all the answers, and I didn't know how to navigate the future without him. But little by little, I started to understand that the void wasn't just a place of loss—it was also a space for transformation.

In the absence of his physical presence, I began to rediscover myself, not as I was before, but as someone who had been shaped by love, by loss, and by the strength to keep moving forward. The person I had been was gone, but in that space, a new version of me was emerging, one that carried Yatin's memory not as a weight, but as a guide.

The confusion, the sense of being lost—it would always be a part of me. But in time, I realized that the future was still mine to shape, even without him beside me.

His love, his spirit, would always be a part of me, and though the void would never truly disappear, it would become a space where I could honor him, where I could find the strength to keep going, even when the path seemed uncertain. And in that uncertainty, I would learn to live again, not as I was, but as someone who had learned to carry love beyond death, into the future that awaited me.

"In the space where love once lived, an endless void remains—a silent echo of all that was and all that will never be."

◆◆◆

Chapter 7 : Finding A New Path In His Memory

In the quiet stillness of the night, a soft breeze whispered through the trees, carrying a faint echo of something familiar. It wasn't a sound, nor a voice, but a presence—a feeling that had once been anchored in the world of the living. Yatin, a name that once brought warmth to the heart, now existed only as an energy, a presence that lingered beyond the horizon.

For the one who was left behind, the absence was a constant ache, but the feeling of Yatin's energy was undeniable. It was like the stars in the night sky, invisible yet ever-present. His laughter, his words, his quiet support—they had not disappeared, but had transformed into something more profound, a force that moved through the universe in ways not yet fully understood.

One evening, as the sun dipped below the horizon, the soul of the one who remained felt a pull. It was not a physical pull, but something deeper, a calling from within. Yatin's energy was alive, woven into the very fabric of the world, and in that moment, it felt as though a new path was opening—one that could be followed not with feet, but with heart.

The path was not a straight line, nor a road marked with signs. It was a journey of discovery, of learning to listen to the unseen and feel the world in a different way. Each step was guided by the energy that Yatin had left behind, like the steady rhythm of a drumbeat that echoed through the air. It was not a path of sorrow, but of transformation.

The first step was simple—quiet reflection. In the stillness, memories of Yatin began to emerge, not as memories in the traditional sense, but as sensations. The feeling of warmth when they had been together, the shared moments of silence that spoke volumes, the deep understanding without words. All of these moments became a source of strength, teaching that Yatin was not truly gone. He was simply somewhere else, part of the energy that flowed through the universe.

As the days passed, the one who was left behind learned to move through life with an open heart, listening for the subtle shifts in the air, the moments when Yatin's energy seemed to guide them toward something new. It wasn't about seeking answers, but about embracing the journey with faith, trusting that the energy of Yatin was always there, nudging them toward growth and change.

And then, one day, as the winds whispered once more, a realization came. The path was not just a journey through life—it was a path to a deeper understanding of the self, of the interconnectedness of all things. Yatin's energy had opened a door, not to another world, but to a new way of seeing this one. It was a path of connection, where the physical and the spiritual intertwined, where the boundaries between life and death were not so distinct.

The one who remained now walked a path with purpose, not in the absence of Yatin, but in the presence of his energy. Every step was a testament to the fact that while Yatin may no longer walk in the physical world, his essence continued to guide, to shape, and to inspire. The path was not defined by loss, but by the enduring power of love and energy that transcended time and space.

"Through the pain of loss, I walk a new path, guided by the light of his love, which forever illuminates my way."

◆◆◆

Chapter 8 : Rediscovering Myself

The world had changed. The vibrant presence of Yatin, the one who had been my rock, my confidant, my partner in every sense, was now gone. Yet, amidst the overwhelming sorrow, there was something else—a faint, distant pulse, a reminder that Yatin's spirit, his energy, still lingered, somehow.

I had always believed that Yatin and I would walk through life together, side by side, raising our children, sharing our dreams, growing old together. But now, I stood at the crossroads of my life, unsure of where to go or what to do. The children, too young to fully understand the loss, looked to me for strength, for comfort, for guidance. Their innocent eyes, full of trust and need, were the spark that ignited something deep within me.

The first few weeks after Yatin’s passing were the hardest. I found myself waking up to a world that felt foreign, like I was walking through someone else’s life. I was overwhelmed by the weight of responsibility. I had always been there to support Yatin, but now the roles had reversed. I had to be strong for the children. I had to step into the role that Yatin had once shared with me, and in doing so, I realized that there was more strength within me than I had ever known.

At first, it was the small things—the daily routines, the decisions Yatin would have made, the simple acts of parenting that now fell solely on my shoulders. I struggled with the weight of it all, unsure if I was doing the right thing, feeling lost in a world without him. But slowly, over time, something shifted. I began to hear Yatin's voice in my thoughts—not in words, but in the way he had always guided me. It was as if his energy had not disappeared, but had transformed, weaving itself into the very fabric of my life.

I remembered the way he used to encourage me to be brave, to trust my instincts, to face challenges head-on. He had always believed in me, even when I didn't believe in myself. And now, as I stood alone, I had to believe in myself too.

The children became my compass. Their needs, their laughter, their moments of joy, and their sorrow—they

pulled me out of my own grief and forced me to keep moving forward. Each day, I took small steps, learning to balance my own healing with their needs. I began to see Yatin in them—in the way they smiled, in the way they held each other close, in the way they cared for me. It was as if his legacy was alive in their hearts.

One day, as I sat with my children in the park, watching them play, I felt a quiet shift within me. The grief, while still there, no longer consumed me. I realized that I was not just surviving; I was growing. I had taken on the mantle of responsibility, but I had also discovered a part of myself I never knew existed. The mother I had always been, yes, but also the woman who could stand on her own, who could face the world with courage, even in the face of loss.

I had found strength I didn't know I had. I had found resilience, compassion, and a deeper love for my children. And I had found a way to carry Yatin's spirit with me—not as a burden, but as a source of strength. His love, his guidance, his unwavering belief in me, still pulsed through my veins, helping me navigate this new path.

In that moment, I understood that Yatin's death was not an end, but a transformation. He had passed on, but his influence, his energy, was a part of me, a part of our family. And as I looked at my children, I knew that together, we would carry his legacy forward. We would honor him, not by clinging to the past, but by living fully in the present, by embracing the responsibilities he had shared with me, and by continuing to grow, together.

And so, I moved forward, one step at a time, rediscovering myself in the process. Each day, I learned to embrace

the challenges, the joys, and the pain. And with each passing day, I became more of the person I was meant to be—strong, loving, and unbreakable, just as Yatin had always known I could be.

"In the ashes of what was, I found the strength to rise anew, a version of myself forged in resilience and reborn in hope."

◆◆◆

Chapter 9 :The Love That Never Fades

In the quiet moments, when the world around me slows down and the noise of everyday life fades into the background, I can still feel him—Yatin. His presence, though no longer visible to my eyes, lingers in the spaces between my breaths, in the rhythm of my heartbeat, in the quiet corners of my soul. Our love was a bond that defied the constraints of time and space, and even death itself couldn't sever it.

Grief came in waves, overwhelming and relentless, but through it all, I held onto the love we shared. I could feel him with me in the quiet moments, in the stillness of the night when the stars seemed to whisper his name. And in my heart, I knew that love doesn't fade. It doesn't die. It transforms, becomes something deeper, something eternal.

Now, I carry him with me—not in the form of a memory, but as a living presence that guides me through each day. When I face challenges, I feel his strength beside me. When I need comfort, I hear his voice in the quietest of moments, telling me that everything will be okay. His
love continues to inspire me, to push me to be better, to be braver, to be kinder.

Yatin's love is a light that never dims, a flame that continues to burn brightly, even in his absence. It is a reminder that love is not bound by the limits of this life, but is something that transcends death itself. His spirit lives on in me, in every choice I make, in every act of kindness, in every moment of strength. And though I can no longer hold his hand or see his smile, I know that his love will forever be my guiding star.

As I move forward in life, I carry his love with me. It is the wind beneath my wings, the steady pulse in my heart. And no matter where life takes me, I will always find him, for love, true love, never fades. It simply transforms, becoming a part of who we are, guiding us through the darkest of times and into the light. Yatin's love is with me, always and forever.

"True love, like the stars, remains constant in the sky—its light enduring, even when unseen, forever shining in the heart."

◆◆◆

A Love Letter To My Heavenly Husband

As I close the final page of this story, I realize that the words on these pages can never fully capture the depth of my love for you, Yatin. You are not just a memory, but a presence that continues to fill my heart. Every moment, every breath, carries the essence of your love, transcending time and space. Though you are no longer here with me in the physical world, you remain with me in ways that words could never express.

You were my partner, my best friend, my love. And even though you are in a place far beyond this earth, I know you are watching over me, guiding me with the same warmth and kindness that you always did. Your love has shaped me in ways I will carry forever.

In this life, we were two souls intertwined, and in the next, I know our love will continue to shine brightly. You are my forever, my angel, my heavenly husband. Until we meet again, I will carry you with me, every step, every day, knowing that our love is eternal.

I love you, now and always Yatin.

A Note To The Reader

Thank you for joining me on this journey through the pages of my heart and soul. But this story, though powerful and raw, is only the beginning. The path I've walked has led me to a place of transformation, where the ashes of my past have become the fuel for my rebirth. In my next book, I will share how I took my life to another level—how I learned to rise from the depths of loss and confusion and find strength in the most unexpected places.

Stay tuned for my another book, for the story isn't over. In fact, it's just beginning.

About The Author

Apurva aspires to leave a legacy of joy and empowerment, aiming to create meaningful changes in society. She dreams of building a world where happiness and abundance are within reach for everyone. She enjoys spending quality time with her family. She believes in maintaining a balanced lifestyle that nurtures both the mind and body, emphasizing authenticity, consistency, and a deep commitment to excellence in all aspects of life.

Through Love Beyond Death, Apurva shares her deeply personal journey of love, loss, and acceptance, hoping to inspire readers to embrace life's unpredictability with grace and gratitude. Ambadnya to Bapu Aai and Dada.Forever Grateful to Mitesh Sir and Indu Mam. Deepest Gratitude to Mom & Dad. Heartfelt Thanks to Yamini and Vaibhav for their unwavering love. Endless Love to Vaijayanti & Aasaavari.

◆◆◆

www.ingramcontent.com/pod-product-compliance
Lightning Source LLC
LaVergne TN
LVHW071131160826
845679LV00005B/1246
* 9 7 9 8 8 9 7 2 4 6 8 2 3 *